A STUDY IN DUST AND ECHOES

BY

Mary Wills

This is under the copy right of Mary Wills.

To reproduce, you must have the express permission of

Mary Wills.

Mary Wills © 2022

THOUGHTS DEVOUR	viii
PRAGMA	x
A STUDY IN DUST AND ECHOES	12
NEVER TELL	14
AN OPEN LOVE LETTER	15
PLEASE DON'T GO	17
FRED	18
WASTING MY YOUNG YEARS	19
DEAREST MARY	20
DEAREST TRAUMA	22
TICK TOCK	23
I'VE BEEN THINKING ABOUT YOU	24
SUNSETS	25
AN OPEN LETTER TO ASEXUALITY	26

Mary Wills © 2022

DARKNESS 27

VILLAIN 29

ACRID 30

AN OPEN LETTER TO ME 33

SOMETIMES 34

THE HALLWAY 35

MORTUARY 37

AN APOLOGY 39

THE MOST INTELLECTUAL POEM EVER 41

BEES 42

RELIEF 44

PROMISE 45

BULLSH*T 46

COWS 47

PORTRAIT 48

PLEASE DON'T GIVE UP...............................49

Mary Wills © 2022

YOU	50
INSOMNIA	51
ENOUGH	52
TO BE HEARD	53
I DO	54
ERASURE	55
TIME	56
ONE, TWO…	57
THE FUTURE IS UNCERTAIN	59
SNAP OUT OF IT	60
RUNAWAY	61
DEAR FATE	62
ATHETIST POEM	63
THE MELODIST	65
NIGHT	66
THE FIVE STAGES OF A VICTIM	67

THE LIES WE TELL 69

SHARP SUITS AND PENCIL SKIRTS 70

HEARD YOU CRY 72

FAIRYTALES 73

OUT OF FOCUS 74

DROWNING 75

NEVER AGAIN 76

AFTERWORD 78

Mary Wills © 2022

Extreme fear can neither fight nor fly

~William Shakespeare

Mary Wills © 2022

THOUGHTS DEVOUR

Thoughts devour me,
All-consuming and suffocating,
Panic sets in like cement,
Surrounding my chest cavity in an iron vice,
I can't do this,
I can't do this,

Want grows stronger,
A want for a better life,
A want to be someone,
But,
Thoughts devour me,
All-consuming and suffocating,
Panic sets in like cement,
I can't do this,
I can't do this,

I can't sleep,
If I do,
It's the constant nightmares,
I can't eat,
If I do,
All I hear is, *you should not eat that,*

Thoughts devour me,
All-consuming and suffocating,
Panic sets in like cement,
I can't do this,
I can't do this,

What if I fail?
What if I break in half?

Mary Wills © 2022

What if I get hurt?
Or lose a part of myself?
What if I move and everything collapses around me?

Thoughts devour me,
All-consuming and suffocating,
I can't do this,
I can't do this,

I cannot govern my emotions,
They rise and swell like an angry sea,
Threatening to pull me back under the surf,
I can't do this.
I can't do this.
But I must,

For if I never try,
I will never forgive myself.

Thoughts devour me,
All-consuming and suffocating,
I can't do this.
I can't do this.
But I must

Mary Wills © 2022

PRAGMA

Standing still in a dimly lit room,
Candles flicker,
The sweet perfume smell of roses and the more bitter tones of wine fill the air,
Soft swell of violin music,
Eyes closed,
Forehead to forehead,
My hand over your heart, feeling the steady rhythm of your heart,

I crave this closeness with another,
Having moments like this,
To be held and feel that everlasting love of pragma,
To feel the warm blanket of safety and love settling over me and you,

A bond so deep it is everlasting, and will transcend space and time,
A bond so deeply committed and everlasting,

But,
I fear I will never have this or find you,
That I will be destined to wanting and longing for the rest of my life,
That I will be still too scared to reach out a hand and ask for you…
That upsets me more than you can imagine,

I fear I will never have this or find you,
I feel no attraction to others,
Never have crushes,

Mary Wills © 2022

I feel unlovable and broken,

My soul yearns for you,
But I am worried,
If I ever find you,
You will turn away.
I feel so unlovable.

A STUDY IN DUST AND ECHOES

I want to shelter myself,
Under the warm blanket of the sign of melody,
Where moonlight shards illuminate the room, and slip over the sleek body of the violin,
Where musings and fears are not the most prominent feature of this room,

But this room is not bathed in moonlight shards,
The sleek body of the violin, is a charred and mangled mess,
The musings and fears have become an all-consuming fire that rages outside the windows.

The fear is burning my fucking world to the ground,
The sign of melody is becoming nothing than a study in dust and echoes,
The fear is all devouring,

No music from the violin fills this air,
No moonlight can penetrate through the red, orange and white flames that scream outside,

Mary Wills © 2022

The room and the shadows are elongated from the flicker of the flames,

Oh, why do I have to be so scared of change?
Why can't I embrace moving with grins and joy?
Oh, why has this made me take a step back in the wrong direction?
Oh, why has the sign of melody become a study in dust and echoes?

When the fear stops consuming me,
I just hope there are enough pieces of me left to pick up,
Have I already lost myself?
Am I doing the right thing?
Or will I become a study in dust and echoes?

I want to shelter myself,
Under the warm blanket of the sign of melody,
Where moonlight shards illuminate and dance around the room,

Where the sleek body of the violin plays music once again,
The notes chasing away the musings and tears,
The notes chasing away the musings and fears,
The notes elevating the musings and hopes,
But instead,
The sign of melody is a study in dust and echoes.

Mary Wills © 2022

NEVER TELL

I felt so disgusting,
Showers did not help to get rid of the feeling of your hands,
I was violated,
Humiliated,
I felt so disgusting,
That I nothing better than object of someone else's eyes,

"You will never tell anyone."
Those are words no sixteen-year-old should ever gave to hear,
Words that made me take another good look at you,
You were never a friend I had known for years,
You were an enemy, biding your time,

Why did you have to pick me?
I was sixteen for two weeks.
I had my whole life ahead of me,
Then suddenly I am not even sure I will make it to eighteen years old,

"You will never tell anyone."
Well…that failed,
I went to the police three days later,
And my answer to you still is:
FUCK YOU.

I will never be silent.
I will scream about this from the roof tops,
Even if I can never mention your name,
I will never be silent.

For silence is complying to what *you want*.

Mary Wills © 2022

AN OPEN LOVE LETTER

You will find out how to love yourself again,
You will stop seeing yourself as the other person,
You will stop seeing yourself as the stranger in the mirror opposite you,

You may feel you have no right to love yourself,
That after everything that has happened to you,
You are disgusting and somehow sullied,
You are not,
You more than anyone has the right to love you,
You are not disgusting or sullied,

I know how tiring it is,
Fighting your thoughts and battling your demons every day,
Struggling to find a reason to wake up in the morning,
Struggling to see a future or even a future where you are alive,
It is an uphill struggle,

One day you will look back on those days and be proud you got through those bleak days,
They will become a study in dust and echoes,
One day you will love yourself,
It may happen gradually,
But it will happen,

You will stop seeing a stranger staring back at you in glass reflections and mirrors,
You will stop wondering if you will ever be good enough,
You will start seeing you and embrace you,

Mary Wills © 2022

These things may take time,

 But one day,
You will find it in yourself,
To love yourself again,
And to stop seeing a stranger.

Mary Wills © 2022

PLEASE DON'T GO

Why are you out of my reach?
Why do you feel an infinity away?
Why is it when I want love and warmth, I get denied?
Why am I so scared to find you?

I am not aromantic,
But asexual,
But I want romance,
The dinners,
The roses,
The whole thing,

It is a conundrum,
I want love and warmth, and to find someone I can marry someone,
Without the other side of things,
I want companionship,
But the fear of being judged is overpowering,

I need you,
But why are you out of my reach?
I want you,
But why do you feel an infinity away?

I will never find you,

But if I do find you,
Please don't go.

Mary Wills © 2022

FRED

This poem is dedicated to 'Fred'. His name is not Fred, but he wanted to be called Fred in this. So…Fred it is. You weirdo. (Not really, I love you).

Have you ever known someone to make bad jokes? Or to send an endless flurry of memes?
Welcome to Fred!

Fred is one of my best friends,
Known each other a long time now,
If you knew Fred, you would be so proud to be his friend,
Fred is one of a kind,

As someone once said: things are never so scary when you got a best friend,
This is certainly true, as my day always brightens when Fred is around,
I will miss you tremendously my dear Fred when I move,

I'll never leave you behind or forget the helicopter boy,
Goodness knows, I can never escape your endless dad jokes and memes,
(Not that I want to escape that is),

You are such a kind soul,
One of the nicest people I know,
Never stop being you,
Or…
 Stop telling your dad jokes.

Mary Wills © 2022

WASTING MY YOUNG YEARS

Wasting my young years,
Acting as if I had not been sexually assaulted,
Wasting my young years,
Staring at walls and watching crime shows,
Wishing I was dead.

Wasting my young years,
Acting as if I was not dying inside,
Wasting my young years,
Curled into a ball of self-loathing,

My teenage years should have ended in failed relationships,
My teenage years should have ended in getting A levels
and joy,
My teenage years should have ended in self-discovery,
My teenage years ended in self harm,
My teenage years ended in wanting to die,

I had my young years wasted,
All because of you,
But no more will I waste my years on the trauma,
Or waste my years on *you*.

Mary Wills © 2022

DEAREST MARY

You left me in the dark,
In the dark shadows of your mind,
In a long corridor with *one florescent light,*
Moaning for you to notice me,
Chained and shackled,

This is not what this was meant to be *used for,*
What was it they called it in school?
Method of Loki is used to *remember things,*
Not lock them away,

You left me in the dark,
In the dark shadows of your mind,
In a long corridor with one florescent light,
Then I heard *you,*

A small *heartbreaking sob,*
That I suppose would break me,
But you chained and shackled me,
In the dark shadows of your mind,

Then I saw you,
Dearest Mary,
All tear stained and dead eyed,
Thin and frail,
A shadow of your former self,
I took the life from your soul,
I took all the smiles and kind words,
That hope you had.
Became nothing.

You left me in the dark,

Mary Wills © 2022

In the shadows of your mind,
In a long corridor with one florescent light,
Moaning for you to notice me,
Chained and shackled,

Demanding that you pay attention to me, your fucking trauma,
How is your life going?
Are you dead-

DEAREST TRAUMA

You tell me I'll be alone,
That I will never be worthy of love,
That no one can ever love someone like me,
A asexual individual,
That they would rather call me freak and other names,

You tell me I'll never get to where I want to be,
You tell me I'll never move,
That I will never be hired,
Someone would be mad to hire a *freak* like me,

Just stop,
I ask you kindly to just stop,
What is your goal *dearest trauma?*
Being asexual is what makes me unique,
If I don't get hired, I will just keep going and *never* stop till someone does hire me,

I am tired of fighting you,
We fought, I was indisposed,
I am tired of fighting you, but that doesn't mean I will *stop*,
You will *never* win again,
My life is not *you,*
My life is so much more than you, my *dearest trauma,*

So do *your best,*
Ask me why I am not dead yet,
Shame me, ridicule me, spit on me, punch me, stab me, *shoot me!*
Rip me apart if you fucking dare.
But it won't be *me* who loses this fight.

Mary Wills © 2022

TICK TOCK

Tick tock.
Flashbacks. Green woodland on one side. Hare jumping across-
Tick tock.
Panic sets in. Breathing is difficult. Pain-
Tick tock.
Please I don't want to see it again-
Tick tock.
Chest begins to feel trapped in an iron vice. I can't breathe. I can't breathe!
Tick tock.
Please stop! I don't want this- why-
Tick tock.
Tick tock.
Tick tock.
I-I can't do this anymore.

I'VE BEEN THINKING ABOUT YOU

I've been thinking about you,
The way you could possibly smile,
And the way your eyes crinkle when you smile,
I've been thinking about you,
Someone I don't know yet, but want to fall in love with,

I've been thinking about you,
The way you could possibly walk,
I've been thinking about you,
What it would be like to wake in the night afraid from a nightmare,
Wondering if you were there, if you would wake up and tell me it was okay,

I like to think we would have moments of spontaneity,
I like to think we would have moments on the top of mountains watching sunsets of the USA,
I like to think we would laugh over stupid things,
Your legs over mine, or my legs over yours as we sit there and laugh,

I've been thinking about you,
I wonder if we will ever meet.

Mary Wills © 2022

SUNSETS

Pale Pink syncs with pastel tangerine across the sky,
Somewhere high above me,
Soars a bird of prey,
Who spies down on me from the sky,

The air is alive and vibrant with flickering fireflies,
The fireflies flicker on and off,
Keen to find a mate,

The mountains are shrouded in pastel pinks, periwinkle blue and tangerine,
The dark green mountains are going to sleep,
The cold and frigid air of February is skin deep,
But I don't care,

The sunset over the mountain is peaceful, elegant, and beautiful,
But even now I long for another to be here with me,
To bask in natures beauty,

I've been thinking about you,
I wonder if we will ever meet.

Mary Wills © 2022

AN OPEN LETTER TO ASEXUALITY

Asexuality is feeling little to no sexual attraction,
I don't get crushes at all,
It makes me feel broken at times,
Like I should be feeling this normal thing, but I just can't,
It feels like I am committing a crime,

But asexuality is what makes me, me,
I am slowly leaning to love this about myself,
To embrace this part of me,
But at times I still wonder if I am broken and pushing myself into a corner,

It is difficult when culture is, so sex orientated,
I have dated,
In attempt to be 'normal',
But it has been abnormal for *me,*
It makes me feel claustrophobic and gasping for air,
Leaves me wondering what the fuck I am doing,

Asexuality is normal,
Asexuality is not abnormal,
I am not hurting someone by not having a relationship,

Never try to be someone you are not,
Who you are is *enough.*

Mary Wills © 2022

DARKNESS

Darkness is beautiful,
Swirling and inky,
With depths you could never want to go too,
Darkness is beautiful, but only if you know to use it well,

The darkness is all-consuming and soul destroying,
But used well and kept at bay,
Can be the most beautiful thing you have ever seen,

For some of us the darkness is thrust upon us,
The darkness leaves a scaly mark and horns on us,
We get accused of being devils,

But,
Either way, whether it has been thrust on you or not,
It is human nature to question the darker side of everything,

To say it is not,
Is to deny yourself a very basic human instinct,

What you do with the darkness is what counts,
Some commit crimes and hurts others,
Letting the darkness within them win,
Some put that darkness into creative mediums,
Some twist that darkness into helping others,
Some mark their bodies with the story of the darkness that was forced upon them,

I mark my body in tattoos,
A story on my skin,
A clash of good and evil,

Mary Wills © 2022

A clash of the moon and sun, then learning to be friends with each other,

I do not see myself as good or bad,
I am not either,
I just choose to do good and use that darkness thrust upon me,
For good,
For the darkness will never win.
I will never be the villain of someone else's story.

Mary Wills © 2022

VILLAIN

I wonder if everyone feels like a monster,
I see myself in a reflection and see a villain,
Someone who is so terrible and has no emotions,
And does not care for others,
But that is not true,
I am also not the villain of my story,

I have been asked,
How would you imagine you would react to a villain? If they went after you?
But I don't have to imagine,

Meeting a villain is not fun or sudden,
You are not suddenly going to start solving crimes, or trying to stop them,
They are not usually well dressed or polite,
Not usually ultra-smart either,

Meeting a villain is not fun or sudden,
Meeting a villain gives you PTSD,
I wake screaming from nightmares,
There are the constant flashbacks,
The constant worry,
The constant distrust of others,

Meeting a villain is not fun or sudden,
It is heart breaking and terror inducing,
Whether knowing you will live or die,

I don't have to imagine what it is like meeting a villain,
I don't even have to imagine how I would react.

Mary Wills © 2022

ACRID

Acrid and dry,
Rustic orange sand crunching under my feet,
I stumble and trudge forward,
There are no streets in sight,
Only barren landscapes,

Slowly,
A figure rises in front of me,
Standing on cracked ground with fissures under his feet,

There he is,
Fox pin on his cream tie,
Uncreased suit,
Prim and proper,
"How are you doing Mary?"

Acrid and dry,
Rustic orange sand crunching under my feet,
I stumble and trudge forward,
There are no streets in sight,
Only barren landscapes dotted with sand dunes and burnt-out trees,
A tongue that is heavy and cracked from no moisture,

"Not good." Is my croaky and horse answer,
He nods and his eyes dart over me in unveiled disgust,
A dry wind crawls over my burnt and charred skin,
Clothes barely hung to me or are imbedded into my burnt flesh,
My hair is gone, burnt away,
I don't even have a right hand,
Just a stump with some sun-bleached bone sticking out,

Mary Wills © 2022

"You look like shit." Is his comment,
In that moment,
All I can do is comment: "Please help! I can't stop the panicking. It is hurting me. *Please help."*
I beg him,
But he just stands there,

Dry and acrid,
Crunching under my feet as I stumble and trudge forward is rustic orange sand,
Stumbling towards him with an outstretched hand,
Here there are no streets in sight,
Sand dunes and burnt-out trees mar the barren place,

He scoffs: "I can't help. You are past help."
No- no- *this is not meant to happen!*
He-he is my comfort,
He helps me,
No! *This is not meant to happen!*

I stare at him unable to cry,
But disbelief in every part of me,
"Cause I am you." He whispers,

A dry and acrid wind crawls over my skin which is burnt and charred,
Some bits of my skin are starting to flake off and become dust and echoes,
Slowly, he dissipates into dust and echoes,

"NO!" I scream,
I can't do this,
I can't do this,
I can't do this,
I can't do this,

Mary Wills © 2022

I can't do this,
I can't do this,
I can't do this,
I can't do this,
I can't do this,
I can't do-

"You can do this." Whispers a new voice in my ear.

AN OPEN LETTER TO ME

I know you are terrified,
You are terrified of moving,
You are terrified you will never get the job you want,
You are terrified you will fail,
You are terrified…you will let your family down,

I know you are panicking,
Panicking about asexuality,
Panicking whether you are good enough to do what you want,

You will get there and be fine,
You will get there and be what you want,
You will get there and find accepting people,
You will get there and be grand,

You can do this,
You can travel to a new country,
You can get the job you want,
You can be who you are,
You can do this Mary,

Just take a deep breath and go for it.

Mary Wills © 2022

SOMETIMES

Sometimes we fall in love with ideas,
Not people,
The ideas we have of people,
That are so closely engrained,

Sometimes we fall in love with ideas,
And forget real life exists,
We want to escape our bleak reality,
Where we may not be accepted for who we are,
To find something more exciting and welcoming,
A façade to protect ourselves,

Sometimes we fall in love with ideas,
That when these ideas fall apart,
We break in half,

Sometimes we fall in love with ideas,
And forget to stop living.

Mary Wills © 2022

THE HALLWAY

You are locked behind a door,
I can hear you screaming for my attention,
Clawing the door,
But I cannot deal with you right now,
He will deal with you,
With his fox pin tie and charming smile,

I slowly turn away,
From a door of claw marks and deep gouges,
To a corridor of splendor and oak panels on the walls,
Cherry and Oak doors lining the seemingly endless hallway,

A figure leans against a wall,
Facing me with crossed arms,
She looks almost bored,
But slightly worried as she looks at me,

I looked behind me,
To the round stain glass window,
Of disjointed pieces of glass, forming no picture-

No,
A picture is forming,
But one I cannot read just yet,
I am not quite ready,

There is periwinkle blue,
Tangerine orange,
Vermillion red,
Yellow ochre,
Disjoined pieces of colour,

Mary Wills © 2022

I turn towards her again,
Standing in the disjointed array of colours glittering down,
As an unknown light source shines through the stain glass window,
"You can do this. Just take a deep breath and go for it." She whispers.

But something deep inside me,
Is withering and screaming,
Telling me:
I can't do this
I can't do this
I can't do this
I can't do this
I can-

"You can do this." She says again more forcefully,
Looking me in the eyes as I take a deep breath,
"I can do this." I whisper.
"Just take a deep breath and go for it."

Mary Wills © 2022

MORTUARY

A deceased person is bizarre and as alien as an alien,
There is no hint as to whom the person was,
No hint as to how they felt in life,

You have moments pause,
As it is so bizarre,
To be stood in front of a deceased person,

I stood there feeling a mix,
From peacefulness to an evenness,
From an evenness to speechlessness,

You have moments pause,
As it is so bizarre,
To be stood in front of a deceased person,

Gloves of blue latex pulled over pale fingers,
Hands in the air staring silently,
An apron of plastic pulled tight around my little black dress,

I really should not have dressed like I was attending a funeral,
Least of all in my best dress,

You have moments pause,
As it is so bizarre,
To be stood in front of a deceased person,

A deceased person,
Cold and lifeless,
Lays on the morgue table of silver,

Mary Wills © 2022

With milky and fallen in eyes,
With a mouth hanging gape,

What am I doing here?
How did I get here?

You have moments pause,
As it is so bizarre,
To be stood in front of a deceased person,

Good work people would say,
But all I can think,
Is how weird it is he has no air in his airways,
How weird it is to be stood here in front of a deceased person,

"Do you want to help dress him?"
My thirty seconds of bizarre emotions are chased away,
I blink a few times,
Take a deep breath and nod,

"Of course." I answer,

The thirty seconds I allowed to be speechless are up,
Now I take the socks,
And put the socks on the deceased.
They were polka dot.

Mary Wills © 2022

AN APOLOGY

I apologize,
To myself,

I am my own worst critic,
I like to say it is cause I am analytical,
But it is not,

I look at myself in the mirror and call myself fat,
I look at myself in a reflection and call myself ugly,
I see my cosplays and cringe away,

I see my writing and tell myself it is shit,
I see my portrait work and point out every flaw,

The future I am scared of,
I am already telling myself I will be a shit person,
I will never get my job,

I am my own worse critic,
I like to say it is cause I am analytical,
But it is not,

I cannot stand myself,
Everything I do is never good enough,
Everything I do I hate,

Oh, when will I feel proud of myself?
Look at what I am achieving,
Oh, Mary when will you learn to love yourself?

I am my own worse critic,
I like to say it is cause I am analytical,

Mary Wills © 2022

But it is not.

Mary Wills © 2022

THE MOST INTELLECTUAL POEM EVER

I'm sorry if I seem uninterested,
I am not interested,
Fuck off please.

BEES

Bees offer honey far more readily than they sting,
Bees only sting when they feel threatened,
And it ends their life,

I was threatened with your lies that day.
"No one will ever believe you."
"You will in trouble if you tell anyone."
"I'll give you things if you do not tell."

But I stung you badly, didn't I?
I went to the police three days later,
You did not expect it,

That is when your harassment started,
More than 180 hours of footage showing you harassing us,
But somehow, it was not enough,
Somehow you were still believed,
Somehow the case was dropped,

You are still doing this shit years later,
I still have to call the police,
Who I do not trust,

I am still fearful of you,
But I will never let you hold this over me,

Bees offer honey more readily than they sting,
Bees only when they feel threatened,
And it ends their life,
Despite you,
And all the harassment and the sexual assault,

Mary Wills © 2022

I will offer honey to those who need it,
I will never sting another person,
I will be better,
But you will never be anything but a sad old man.

Mary Wills © 2022

RELIEF

There was a relief in the storms approach,
A calmness that always predates a storm,
A calmness that settled over my shoulders,

I stood in the dark holding a candle in a candleholder,
The candle nearly gone,
I cupped my hands around the flickering flame,
The window frames started to rattle loudly and violently,

Then bellowing through the cracks was dust and echoes,
Dust and echoes of anxiety and apprehension,
Anxiety and apprehension trying to extinguish my last flicker of hope,

There is relief in the storms approach,
Even though it brings anxiety and apprehension about the future,
I also know it will banish all those insecurities,

So,
There is relief in the storms approach.

Mary Wills © 2022

PROMISE

Promise me Mary,
Promise me something,

Promise me that you will do your best,
That no matter what,
You will never give up,

Promise me you will be the best version of yourself,
That you will never stop growing to be the best human possible,
That no matter what,
You will never give up,

Promise me,
Promise me no matter what,
You will stay strong.

Promise me Mary.

BULLSH*T

They say things happen for a reason,
Or they were meant to happen,
That you should realize this and accept it,
I say that is a *load of bullshit,*

The only reason what happened happened,
Was because of someone else thinking they had a *right to me,*
That isn't meant to happen,
That isn't fate,
That is *bullshit,*

Stop telling victims,
These things happen for a reason,
It is victim blaming,
It is bullshit.

Mary Wills © 2022

COWS

Stomp. Stomp.
Chew. Stomp.

Oh, what it must be like to be a cow!
Without a worry in the world,
Chewing on lush grass,
Sleeping when you want,
Being around friends,

Oh, what it must be like to be a cow!
It must not be lonely,
Surrounded by a herd,
Oh, So carefree too!
Never stressing of where your next meal may come from,
Or worrying what others think of you,

Oh, what it must be like to be a cow!

PORTRAIT

The scrape of pencil on paper,
The black flowing lines from the lead,
Slowly,
Ever so slowly a face is forming,

Nothing else matters in the world,
But in that moment,
Finishing the portrait,

Shadows deepen,
Highlights blaze,
Everything is in black and grey,

I can spend hours,
Days,
Months,
On a single portrait,
Shading,
Highlighting,

The scrape of pencil on paper,
The black flowing lines from the lead,
Slowly,
Ever so slowly a face is forming.

Mary Wills © 2022

PLEASE DON'T GIVE UP

Please don't ever give up,
Or give into that voice,

I know it can feel like the world is against you,
That no one cares,
That everything is too much to handle,
That your whole life is collapsing around you,
That there is no end to the pain,

You are not alone,
There is always someone who will understand,
You don't have to carry this pain around just on your shoulders,
You are never alone,

Please don't ever give up,
Or give into that voice,
There is no one as unique as you,
There is no other you,
There is no one as strong as you,

Please don't give up.

Mary Wills © 2022

YOU

If I had my way,
I would never move from this moment,

Wrapped in warm blankets and your arms,
Watching you sleep so peacefully,
Calm and beautiful in that moment,

I move your hair from your face,
I must be the luckiest person in the world,

Your eyes open ever so slightly,
Glazed over with sleep,
Then a small smile tugs the corner of your mouth up,
You look down at me,
And I grin to you,
"What a pleasant way to-"

Then I wake up.

INSOMNIA

Night blurs together,
Owl's hoot outside my window,
Staring at a ceiling in the pitch black,
Wondering when I can finally start to feel normal,

Mary, you better watch yourself,
You could seriously fail,
Hello to the demon that is my brain,

I turn on my side,
As if this will help,
Sleep is far away,
Out of my reach,
The day stubbornly out of my reach,

Is time purposely moving slower?
Does time want to torture me?

I stare at the music stand shrouded in blackness,
A red-hot scalds and cascades down my face,
Mary, you know moving to the USA is a coward move,
You can't outrun your demons,
And you can't outrun your past,

I twist roughly back onto my back,
Wide eyes crying silently,
Staring at a ceiling,
Dawn still rises,
Slowly.
Stubbornly.

Mary Wills © 2022

ENOUGH

I've had enough,
I've had enough of never feeling worthy,
I've had enough of *being like this,*
So entwined in trauma,
So engrained in fear,
A slave to the negative emotions swirling around my brain,

Can you not see *I've had enough?*
I am exhausted,
Mentally drained,
Physically exhausted,

I've had enough of being like this,
Beaten down,
Ripped apart,
Scalded,
I've just had *enough,*

I've had enough of the constant fear,
The constant fear I will fail and fall flat on my face,
I want to be proud of myself,
Turn my face to sun and feel the warmth,
I've had enough feeling the cold rays of the moon,

I don't want to be wrapped in a ball of panic,
Never feeling good enough,

Please,
I've had enough.

Mary Wills © 2022

TO BE HEARD

I wanted to be heard,
I wanted to be listened too,
I wanted to be understood,

Expect I was met with ridicule and scorn,
I was met with *'well this isn't as bad as it could have been.'*
It was as bad as it could have been,
It left me with PTSD,

I was left with this somehow being my fault,
That I asked for it,

I never wanted this to happen to me,

You are the justice system,
Why did you let me down so badly?
I was sixteen years old,

I went to you for your help,
To be heard,
To be listened too,

But all I got was ridicule and scorn.

Mary Wills © 2022

I DO

"I do."
Words I so desperately wish to say,
Words I so fear I will never get to say,

Ever since a child,
I have dreamt of the dress,
Dreamed of sharing a day so exquisite and romantic with another,
Dreamed of being that special person to another,
Celebrating that love,

But I feel I won't ever get that,
That I won't ever find the softness of love,
To stare into another's eyes,

To be asexual and want love,
Is starting to feel like getting blood from a stone,

"I do."
Words I so desperately wish to say,
Words I fear I will never say.

ERASURE

"You can't be asexual. You don't look asexual."
Oh, I am sorry,
Do you want me to tattoo asexual across my forehead?

"No. You aren't asexual."
Oh, I am sorry,
I did not realize you knew me better than I knew myself,

I am *asexual,*
I am not broken,
Though I may feel broken at times,
I am valid,
Though I may feel invalid at times,

I am *asexual,*
I am not yours to try and 'fix',
There is nothing broken about me,

An asexual person does not need to validate who they are to you,
An asexual person does not need erasure,
Not when we face a lot of erasure as it is,
I just want to be *accepted,*

I just want someone who understands,
Who will love me for me,
Who will love that I am asexual,
Who won't run and hide,

I just want to be accepted,
And loved for me.

Mary Wills © 2022

TIME

It feels like time is running out,
It feels as if the clocks are turning faster,
I feel as if my life has passed me by,
But I am only twenty-four years old,

It feels as if time is moving too slowly,
But then it also feels as if time is moving too quickly,
And the years are blurring together,
Or the years are not moving at all,

This move feels sudden and disjointed,
Terrifying and alien,

The change in my life feels like a tsunami wave slamming into me,
It feels as if time is running out,

But I am only twenty-four years old,
I have my whole life ahead of me,
But it feels like time is running out.

Mary Wills © 2022

ONE, TWO…

It feels like one breath,
And I will fall apart,

Why do I have to be so scared of change?

It feels like two steps,
And I will turn into dust and echoes,

Why do I have so panicked about moving?

It feels like three sleeps,
And I will never wake up again,

Why do I have to feel like death incarnate?

It feels like four weeks of being in the USA,
And I could utterly fail,

Why do I have to feel like this is a mistake?

One,
Two,
Three,
Four,
Calm down Mary,

One,
Two,
Three,
Four,
Take a deep breath Mary,

Mary Wills © 2022

One,
Two,
Three,
Four,
You can do this Mary.

THE FUTURE IS UNCERTAIN

The future is uncertain,
A big scary and wide unknown,
With infinite possibilities and outcomes,

I wonder who my friends would be,
Will I make friends?
Will my colleagues like me?
Or will I be a hermit?

The thought of getting behind the wheel of a car,
Fills me with apprehension and terror,
Will I be safe?
Will I be a good driver?
Can I do it?

The thought of moving,
Fills me with guilt and terror to my core,
But I know I will do it,

The future scares me,
The unknown scares me,
I don't like not knowing,

The future may be uncertain,
I may not like not knowing,
But change is also a good thing,
This is a *good thing*.

Mary Wills © 2022

SNAP OUT OF IT

Snap out of it,
Why can't you see how good your future is?
How bright and vibrant it is?

Snap out of it,
Don't let the panic win,
Don't let the bad days take over,

Snap out of it,
The trauma is getting less,
The trauma won't ever leave,
But it won't win either,
Not anymore,

Snap out of it Mary,
And start to see,
How amazing you will be.

RUNAWAY

Sometimes I want to run away,
To escape this life,
To feel the soft earth of a forest beneath my toes,
To listen to the rustle of leaves in a breeze,
To hear the sings of birds,

Sometimes I want to sail away on a vast ocean,
To listen to the sounds of crashing waves against the side
of a boat,
To hear the shrill scream of a seagull flying high above,
To taste the salt of the ocean upon my lips,

Sometimes I want to walk among sand dunes,
To feel the hot and scorching breeze on my skin,
To hear the crunch of sand beneath my feet,
To feel the unbearably scorching hot sun beating down
upon my face,

I want to feel like I am living,
A living and breathing thing,
Who has adventures in the great wild world,

Because sometimes I feel I am not living at all,
But slowly becoming dust and echoes,
And I just want to feel alive.

Mary Wills © 2022

DEAR FATE

Dear Fate,
Fuck you,
Yours sincerely,
Mary Wills

P.S
Fuck off.

ATHETIST POEM

When I was fifteen,
Being a nun seemed like a swell career plan,
Now I cringe and laugh,
Oh, thank fuck I never did that,

When I as sixteen,
I lost all respect in God,
Asking: God why me? I live by your rules, and this is the second bad thing to happen to me,
What did I do?

Then it slowly dawned,
God was not real,
I was praying to fiction,
God was never with me,

God *was* a constant in my life,
Omnipresent and omnipotent,
God *was* the light and hope,

Then God lost all meaning,
Heaven and hell became fiction,
An afterlife used to keep me in line,
I grew tired of religion,
And all the rules,

Now instead of saying: God is my constant light,
I say,
God is dead,
Such as Nietzsche says,

Now I live for me,

Mary Wills © 2022

Not for some false hope of a God saving me,
Of being able to attend heaven when I am deceased,

When I was fifteen,
A nun as a career plan seemed like a swell idea,
Now I cringe away,

At twenty-four,
I have learnt my life should not be defined by a God,
Who may or may not be real,
But by how I treat others,
It should be defined,
How I want my life defined.

(P.s, I have nothing against anyone who wishes to be religious. I find religions very interesting and love to learn about them).

Mary Wills © 2022

THE MELODIST

The soft swell of the musical notes,
Cut through the hustle and bustle of a London tube station,
Tapering off and starting again,
Nothing else matters in that moment,
But the melodist,

When panic rises like a rising tide,
Threatening to suck me under and drown me,
I know you will be there,
The melodist,

A violin is melody, beauty, and grace,
Elegance and promise of a melodist kiss upon your lips,
A violin is gossamer, and all things enticing,
A violin is the melodist,

You are what quietens my screaming brain,
For there is nothing more therapeutic than you,
The melodist,

On the darkest and dreariest of days,
When the rain lashes down windows,
And the wind is howling for attention,
I know you are there,
Ready and waiting,
The melodist.

Mary Wills © 2022

NIGHT

The stars are plucked from the night sky,
Spinning and disintegrating as they tumble towards the earth,
I try to catch them and put them back,
But they burn my fingers,

The night sky is collapsing,
The stars blinking out one by one,
Everything is tumbling into a black hole,
I watch as the earth is ripped apart,
There is nothing I can do,

That is how depression feels,
You try and ease the pain,
It feels like it burns you,

That is how depression feels,
A might black hole,
You can never escape from,
Ripping everything apart you hold dear,

But you can get through it,
You can get through it and make it to the other side,
I believe in you.

Mary Wills © 2022

THE FIVE STAGES OF A VICTIM

Embarrassed,
How did I let this happen?
I *should* have stopped it,

Guilt,
I did not do enough to protect others from them,
I *should* have done more,
I *could* have done more,

Anger,
How fucking dare someone feel they have the right to do this to me!
Why the fuck did this *happen* to me?!

Denial,
This *didn't* happen to me,
I am *not* a victim,

Confusion,
Did that happen to me?
Or did I *make* that up?

The five stages of a victim,
Of course,
it is more for some,
And of course,
It is different for all,
For no one is the exact same,

You should *never* feel embarrassed,
You were vulnerable,
This was against your choice,

Mary Wills © 2022

The *person* who did this *should be embarrassed*,

Never let the guilt override you,
If you told- *that is enough,*
If you have not told- *that's okay,*
At the end of the day,
You have yourself to protect,
It is *not* your duty to protect others,

The anger is normal,
You need to let it burn,
Bright and hot,
What happened,
Should *never* have happened,
Let that anger burn,

Denial is normal,
You *don't* want to think this happened to you,
You want to act as if it did not,
Unfortunately, it did,

The confusion over events is normal,
Did I make that up?
Did I make that detail up?
What actually happened?
Why can't I remember this detail?
Trauma is not straight forward and clean cut,
Trauma is messy and confusing,

How you feel is not wrong,
How you feel is valid,
And,
Who you are,
Is not determined by trauma or,
Another's actions.

Mary Wills © 2022

THE LIES WE TELL

I'm okay,
I will get over it,
It's not a massive problem,
I am not worried,
I am not scared,
I am okay,
I am oka-
I am ok-
I am o-
I am-

I am not okay,

Please don't look to closely,
The truth of how I feel,
Is so much starker and bleak,

With short roads and dead ends,
With twists and turns,
The truth of how I feel,
Is so much starker and bleak,

It's easier to spin a lie,
To weave lies around a truth,
Then it is to say the cold hard truth,

The lies we tell,
Are not what we feel,
Please don't look to closely,
I don't want you to see the demons inside.

Mary Wills © 2022

SHARP SUITS AND PENCIL SKIRTS

Sharp suits and cuff links,
Ties and shined brogues,
Tie pins and blank eyes,

Quick wit and tired smiles,
I raise my hand and you follow suit,
I tilt my head to the side, and you follow suit,

Who are you?
Why do you follow my actions?

Pencil skirts with low cut shirts,
Perfectly done red lipstick,
To scare the men and boys alike,

I bring my mouth into a smile,
You follow suit,
I lower my eye lashes,
You follow suit,

Who are you?
Why are you coping me?

Sharp suits and pencil dresses,
Tired smiles with red lipstick,

I know who you are,
You are not some stranger opposite me,

I raise my hand,
You do so in the mirror,
This is meant to be me,

Mary Wills © 2022

But why do you feel so far out of my reach?
Like you are impossible feat,
And all I feel I am doing right now,
Is playing dress up,

I saw you in the mortuary,
All professionalism and no nonsense,

I saw you in the mortuary,
When the detachment went up,
All professionalism and no nonsense,

Why do you feel so far out of my reach?
With your sharp suits and red stained smiles,
Like you are impossible feat,
With your pencil skirts and detachment,

And,
Will I see you again?

Mary Wills © 2022

HEARD YOU CRY

I heard you cry,
Again, last night,

I heard you cry,
You tried to sob quietly,
But like a black eye,
It stood out,

I wanted to reach out,
And tell you it gets better,
Because it *does* get better,

But you are so far out of my reach,
It would be quite a way for me to preach,

I heard you cry,
Again, last night,
You tried to sob quietly,
I wanted to reach out,
But you are so far out of my reach.

Mary Wills © 2022

FAIRYTALES

"What do you want to be when you are older Mary?"
An eight-year-old Mary wanted to be a faerie,
With glistening glitter wings and gossamer gowns,
Magic wands and sprinkling glitter and mayhem,

But through the fairytales,
Through the dragon scales and chain mail,
Of sword waving heroes and villainesses with castles,
Were the trails I wanted to follow,
Not the trail I follow now,
It's a hard pill to swallow,

But we did it,
Eight-year-old Mary!
We became the author you wanted.
Just not in the way you wanted.

OUT OF FOCUS

Seasons pass in a blur,
Green leaves turning to red and brittle leaves,
Red and brittle leaves turning to brown and decaying,

But I never saw this,
I never saw the leaves change with each passing season,
I was lost in a black mist of trauma,

Everything was out of focus,
My life was in a defocus,
Putting everything out of balance,

Days blur together,
Time runs faster without any meaning,
People grow older and disappear,
But I stay the same,

Everything was out of focus,
Everything was out of balance,
Lost in a black mist of trauma.

Mary Wills © 2022

DROWNING

Drowning is so easy,
Living is so hard,

Drowning is so easy,
Letting the trauma win is so easy,

To let yourself sink beneath the ink black waves,
To let those waves, rush down your throat into your lungs,
Drowning is so easy,
Why should I try to live?
If drowning is so easy?

It is easy to forget,
To let the trauma consume you whole,

It is easy to forget,
You have aspirations and dreams,
Drowning is so easy,

Don't ever give in,
You must battle against those inky black waves,
Living is so hard,
But worth fighting for,

The bad days may seem like they are winning,
And drowning will be so much easier than to keep living,
But those days won't win,

Please don't give in.

Mary Wills © 2022

NEVER AGAIN

I kept whispering: "Take a deep breath and go for it."
Till my lips cracked and blood started to run down my chin,
While the panic gripped me in a fiery throng,

The panic screamed around me,
A fiery inferno of flames licking the walls,
Kissing and scorching my skin till it blackened and charred,
But I kept on whispering: "Take a deep breath and go for it."

The panic of moving was not going to win this battle,
The panic,
The trauma,
Was NEVER going to win anymore battles,

Blood runs down my chin,
Thick metallic smell of iron fills the air,
But I kept on whispering: "Take a deep breath and go for it."

Slowly, the room returns to normal,
As the panic screams in protest and I begin to yell those words,
Slowly ever so slowly,
My arms turn to normal,
The skin reknits itself together as I stagger onto my feet screaming those words,

The panic will never win,
The trauma will never win,
The fiery inferno screams around me,
But a bigger and angrier fire burns in my soul,

Mary Wills © 2022

I will move,
I will get my job,
And never ever again,
Will the trauma get the *best of me.*

Mary Wills © 2022

AFTERWORD

I tried my best to make this a lot longer than my last, but it felt right to end the book here with the last being: *and never again, will the trauma get the best of me.*

  It felt natural.

This book only took me less than a week to create. The Sign of Melody took me from February 2022 to September 2022. In turn, my first novel is still being wrote from February.

  I cannot explain why I turned this book out so quickly. But I did.

  I want to thank everyone who reads my books. I know this poem book is not easy to read, hence why I have put a few funny poems in it. But thank you so much for reading and purchasing. It means the absolute world to me.

  Here is to the future!

~Mary Wills

Mary Wills © 2022

Lightning Source UK Ltd.
Milton Keynes UK
UKHW022155090123
415068UK00015B/1827